# Stirling Castle

*Richard Fawcett*

*Principal Inspector of Ancient Monuments*

HISTORIC SCOTLAND

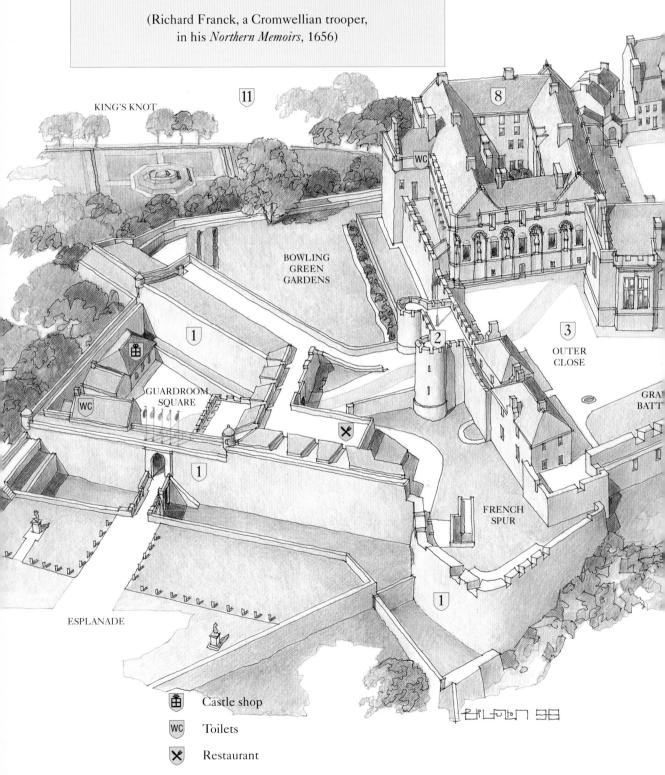

'So let us pass...to the ports of Sterling; where stands a
beautiful and imbellished Castle, elevated on the precipice
of an impregnable rock, that commands the vallies
(as well as the town) and all those habitable parts about it...'

(Richard Franck, a Cromwellian trooper,
in his *Northern Memoirs*, 1656)

KING'S KNOT

11

8

WC

BOWLING
GREEN
GARDENS

1

2

3

OUTER
CLOSE

GUARDROOM
SQUARE

WC

GRAN
BATT

1

FRENCH
SPUR

1

ESPLANADE

Castle shop

WC   Toilets

Restaurant

# A Guided Tour

NETHER
BAILEY

This tour suggests a sequence of viewing the castle, starting and ending at the Outer Defences ①. Now is an exciting time to be visiting the castle since there is currently probably more work in progress than at any time since the late 1500s. This activity is concentrated on the buildings around the Inner Close ④, the main royal enclave, and is aimed at allowing the original qualities of these buildings to be more fully appreciated. Because of these works, it is regretted that not all parts of the castle may be accessible at all times.

Please, never hesitate to ask one of our castle stewards if you wish to know more.

# ① The Outer Defences

The castle is approached across the Esplanade, an area of ground kept open in order to allow the castle's defenders a clear view of those who came near; it was laid out as a parade ground in 1809. Beyond the Esplanade the castle presents a severely plain front on this, its most vulnerable side. Most of what is seen was built between 1708 and 1714, to the designs of Theodore Dury, as a functional barrier against artillery attack. Its low-set, massively constructed walls with pepper-pot sentry boxes at the angles, and its deep ditch with a single entry point across a drawbridge, were ideal for this purpose. The front is defended by a flanking battery, and there were originally two caponiers (firing galleries) within the ditch, though only one remains.

Within the work of 1708-14, the northern (right) half of the Outer Defences incorporates work of the 1550s, built for Queen Mary of Guise, Mary Queen of Scots' mother. The higher section of wall to the right of the gate is one of the faces of what had been a large triangular spur, and a section of its curved prow remains to the right of the gateway.

*One of the eighteenth-century sentry boxes on the Outer Defences.*

*The initials of Queen Anne (Anna Regina) on the keystone of the Inner Gate.*

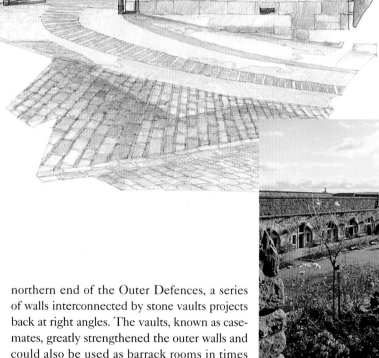

The French Spur, a flanking battery at the far north end of the wall, with two tiers of emplacements firing across the face of the outer wall, is also basically of the 1550s, though the emplacements were originally deeply recessed (see the photograph and reconstruction drawing on page 39). At the southern (left) end of the front, the wall projecting out towards the esplanade is a relic of Dury's original intention simply to build an enclosing wall around what is now the Esplanade. He was ordered to abandon this scheme. Set back beyond the southern end of the Outer Defences, is a three-bay cannon emplacement which defended the less steep ground here.

Within the Outer Defences is a defensive pocket known as the Guardroom Square, overlooked by higher walls. From here an inner gate, which has the cipher of Queen Anne on its keystone, leads through into the castle. This gate was reached across a second ditch which, like the outer ditch, used to be defended by caponiers. Within the square are a guardroom, a stable and a straw store, parts of which were built in 1813; the straw store now houses the shop. Behind the inner walls around the square, and also behind the higher wall at the

northern end of the Outer Defences, a series of walls interconnected by stone vaults projects back at right angles. The vaults, known as casemates, greatly strengthened the outer walls and could also be used as barrack rooms in times of emergency. Those behind the Guardroom Square, which overlook the Bowling Green Gardens, are single-storeyed, and now contain an introductory display. Those behind the northern end of the Outer Defences were originally two-storeyed, and now contain the castle restaurant.

*The casemates overlooking the Bowling Green Gardens.*

A shot-hole in the gatehouse.

The gatehouse with the
Prince's Tower, on the far left.

# ② The Forework

It is likely that, before the mid-sixteenth century, the outer defensive wall across the main approach to the castle always ran on the line of the Forework, and evidence for an earlier wall is still visible in stretches of its lower masonry. The present Forework was built for James IV in the years around 1500, and the master-masons involved were probably John Yorkston and John Lockhart.

The main elements of the design were: a central gatehouse with three gateways and with three-quarter-round towers at all four angles; half-round towers a short distance to each side of the gatehouse; and rectangular towers at the outer ends of the curtain wall (see the reconstruction drawing on pages 34 - 35). From the north-eastern end of the Forework a curtain wall ran back along that side of the castle to meet the North Gate.

The Forework has been frequently modified. The gateway only rises to about a third of its full height, since its upper parts were probably damaged in the siege of 1651, and the existing battlements were built in 1810. The two half-round towers flanking the gateway are largely destroyed, and the Elphinstone Tower, at the north-eastern end, was reduced to half of its height in about 1689 to allow the Three Gun Battery to be formed. The only parts which still reflect the original design are the Prince's Tower, at the south-western end, and the adjoining section of curtain wall.

*One of the two pedestrian entries through the gatehouse, still with its iron portcullis in place.*

When it was complete, however, with its crenellated wall-walks and tall conical roofs, and probably with limewashed walls and coloured carvings, the Forework must have been a wonderful sight. In its design James IV clearly wanted to create far more than just a utilitarian defensive barrier; anyone approaching his castle could have been in no doubt that its lord was of the very highest standing and the longest lineage. Is it even possible that there is a hint of historical romanticism in this design for a king who loved the pageantry of chivalry, and who was fascinated by the Arthurian legends?

*The guns of the Grand Battery.*

# ③ The Outer Close

The Outer Close is the lower of the two principal courtyards of the castle. It is dominated by the Palace to the west and by the gable of the restored Great Hall to the north. On the south side of the close are the handsome late eighteenth-century Main Guard House and the early nineteenth-century Fort Major's House. At the far north end, beyond the Grand Battery of 1689 and adjacent to the North Gate, is the Master Gunner's House, which dates back to the seventeenth century, though it has been extensively remodelled.

Behind the Main Guard House is the surviving part of the Elphinstone Tower. A modern stairway leads down into its two lower floors, which were re-opened in 1921. At the far end of the Grand Battery, in front of the Master Gunner's House, is the stair leading down into the Great Kitchens (see page 16).

*The Main Guard House* (left) *and the Fort Major's House* (right).

# ④ The Inner Close

The Inner Close is reached by a steeply sloping road from the Outer Close, which runs between the Palace and Great Hall, below the early nineteenth-century bridge interconnecting the two buildings. The Close was the great square around which the main royal buildings of the castle were grouped, and archaeological investigations have suggested that it began to take form in the years around 1500, as part of the plans of James IV.

Before then several of the buildings in this part of the castle were set on a diagonal axis, following the natural configuration of the castle rock. The only building which survives on this earlier axis is a much reduced block behind the stair to the Governor's Apartment in the Palace. Burials found within this building indicate that it was one of the two chapels known to have existed within the castle. On the opposite side of the Close, foundations which have been found running partly below the Chapel Royal of 1594 and which are marked out in the paving, were on a parallel alignment to that building. These are thought to have been of the Chapel predating the one we now see; thus there may once have been two chapels set parallel to each other on opposite sides of this area.

*The bridge connecting the Great Hall and the Palace.*

# ⑤ The King's Old Building

Set on the highest part of the castle rock, with magnificent views out to the west, the range known as the King's Old Building was undoubtedly designed for a highly prestigious purpose. Recent investigations strongly suggest that it was the 'King's House', under construction for James IV in 1496, to the designs of Walter Merlioun. It is an L-shaped structure, incorporating earlier walls at its south end, and extended at its north end by Robert William Billings after a fire in 1855. The main rooms were on the first floor, and were approached by a spiral stairway in an entrance tower capped by an octagonal superstructure.

These main rooms originally rose the full height of the building, above the vaulted ground floor, with large windows towards the Inner Close. The stair opened into the king's hall, beyond which was his chamber, with lesser chambers or closets in the cross-wing at the northern end. A room at the south end of the hall was perhaps a kitchen, and there may have been timber galleries in front of the kitchen and at the north end of the chamber (see reconstruction drawing on page 35).

In the course of the seventeenth, eighteenth and nineteenth centuries, the building was extensively subdivided by inserted floors and walls and smaller windows replaced the original larger openings. In its later phases it provided accommodation for officers and the Governor, though in 1855 a panelled museum room was created in the part traditionally (but wrongly) said to have been where the eighth Earl of Douglas was killed by James II (see page 31). The building now houses the regimental museum of the Argyll and Sutherland Highlanders.

*The memorial to the Argyll and Sutherland Highlanders on the Castle Esplanade. Stirling Castle was their depot until 1964.*

# ⑥ The Chapel Royal

It is likely that the main chapel of the castle was always close to the site of the present chapel, and excavation has discovered traces of two earlier buildings on a slightly different alignment. The alignment of the second of these had the disadvantage that it obscured the entrance to James IV's Great Hall. Therefore, it was probably intended to shift the Chapel to its present position soon after 1500, when the Great Hall was nearing completion and the collegiate Chapel Royal was being established within the building which then existed. James IV's

*The imposing entrance into the Chapel Royal.*

death in 1513 probably prevented this rebuilding, though a report of 1583 for James VI strongly recommended that the Chapel should be rebuilt on its present site. This was eventually done in 1594, to provide a setting for the baptism of James VI's first son, Prince Henry. The designer may have been William Schaw.

The Chapel is a large rectangular building entered through an imposing doorway within a triumphal arch surround, and with three paired windows within semi-circular arches on each side of the doorway. Both the doorway and the windows were clearly inspired by prototypes in Renaissance Italy, and

show how strong the influence of such ideas was in Scotland at that time. The Chapel was extensively redecorated by Valentine Jenkin in 1628-9 in preparation for Charles I's visit of 1633, and externally faint traces of painted decoration between the window heads are still visible. The best surviving example of this phase of decoration is the frieze around the interior, which shows the Honours of Scotland (the coronation regalia) between elaborate festoons, and with a painted window in the west gable. Much of what is now seen internally dates from restoration after internal partitions and floors were removed in the 1930s; the timber ceiling was constructed in 1996.

*The interior of the Great Hall looking towards the dais, or high table.*

# [7] The Great Hall

Stirling's Great Hall, the largest ever built in Scotland, was intended for great celebrations and occasions of state. It was nearing completion in 1503. Because of the slope of the land it is set above a vaulted undercroft, which raises the main floor to the level of the Inner Close. There was originally a sunken area covered by a lean-to roof in front of the Hall, on the side towards the Close, but its lower part was vaulted over in the sixteenth century (and by the early eighteenth century the area within the lean-to roof had been enclosed by solid walls).

The Hall is a vast rectangular space, entered from the northern end of the side towards the Close, where there is a screened-off service area. Most of the windows are placed high in the walls, but at the south end a pair of projecting full height bay windows give particular prominence to the dais for the high table. The dais was eventually connected to the Palace by a bridge. The Hall was heated by five fireplaces, two in each of the side walls and one on the dais, and four spiral staircases connect the various levels. The plan of the hall may suggest that one source of inspiration was the hall built for Edward IV (1461-83) of England at Eltham Palace, south-east of London.

In 1964, Stirling Castle ceased to function as a military depot. Shortly thereafter, it was decided the Great Hall should be restored to something like its former glory. At that time, the hall was subdivided into three floors of redundant barrack accommodation. Slowly and painstakingly, the partitions were removed and evidence gleaned for the restoration. Over the past few years the stonemasons have gradually repaired the walls and replaced the missing architectural details. In 1997, the new hammerbeam roof was put into place and in 1999 the walls were rendered and lime-washed on the basis of surviving evidence. The hall can now be seen as intended by its designers in about 1500.

*The restored Great Hall from the Outer Close.*

# ⑧ The Palace

The Palace, built for James V to house himself and his French queen, is the most prominent building within the castle, with magnificent façades towards both the Inner and Outer Closes and a third overlooking the western section of the Forework. Timbers in the building have indicated a commencement date of about 1538 and, since the King's Principal Master of Works, Sir James Hamilton of Finnart, came to the castle in 1537-8, this was presumably to supervise the start of operations. The designer was probably one of the King's French masons, who included Nicholas Roy, John Roytell and Mogin Martin.

There were earlier buildings on the site, parts of which are incorporated in the basement and within the west quarter, though our understanding of the west side is incomplete since part of it collapsed towards the end of the sixteenth century. Nevertheless, the Palace gives an appearance of strict regularity, being planned as a quadrangular building around a central courtyard (the Lion's Den).

The entrance, off the top end of the Inner Close, was originally covered by a large porch, but this was rebuilt on a smaller scale when the stair to the Governor's apartment on the upper floor was constructed in the early eighteenth century. The porch opens onto a gallery inter-connecting the lodgings for the king and queen, which also gives access to the Lion's Den. Each lodging consisted of a Guard Hall, a Presence Chamber and a Bed Chamber, with small Closets off the last room. The king's Closets overlooked the courtyard, while the queen's were in a demolished range behind the Forework.

The queen's lodging had the added benefit of a raised walkway behind the Forework wall. The decoration of the rooms was carefully graded according to their importance and, although only the carved fireplaces now survive in place, we know that at least one of the king's rooms had a panelled ceiling incorporating the superb carved oak roundels known as the Stirling Heads. These roundels were the work of several carvers, amongst whom may have been Robert Robertson, Andrew Mansioun and John Drummond. There are now plans to recreate the appearance of the interiors,

*One of the famous Stirling Heads.*

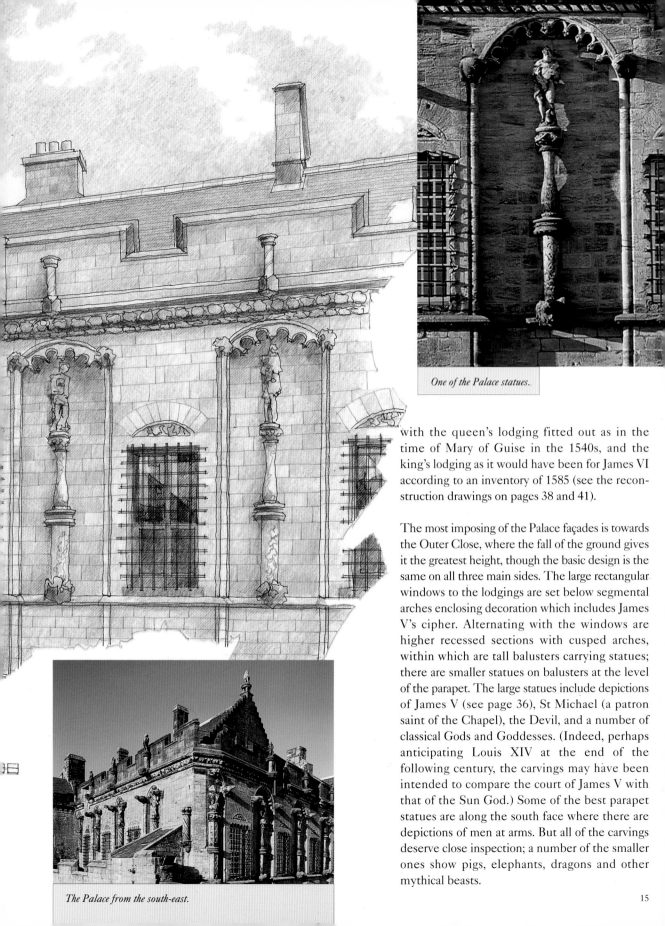

One of the Palace statues.

The Palace from the south-east.

with the queen's lodging fitted out as in the time of Mary of Guise in the 1540s, and the king's lodging as it would have been for James VI according to an inventory of 1585 (see the reconstruction drawings on pages 38 and 41).

The most imposing of the Palace façades is towards the Outer Close, where the fall of the ground gives it the greatest height, though the basic design is the same on all three main sides. The large rectangular windows to the lodgings are set below segmental arches enclosing decoration which includes James V's cipher. Alternating with the windows are higher recessed sections with cusped arches, within which are tall balusters carrying statues; there are smaller statues on balusters at the level of the parapet. The large statues include depictions of James V (see page 36), St Michael (a patron saint of the Chapel), the Devil, and a number of classical Gods and Goddesses. (Indeed, perhaps anticipating Louis XIV at the end of the following century, the carvings may have been intended to compare the court of James V with that of the Sun God.) Some of the best parapet statues are along the south face where there are depictions of men at arms. But all of the carvings deserve close inspection; a number of the smaller ones show pigs, elephants, dragons and other mythical beasts.

# ⑨ The Great Kitchens & North Gate

The early sixteenth-century Great Kitchens, which served the Great Hall, were built against the curtain wall on the north-east side of the Outer Close, though what we see is just a part of what there once was. The vaults over them were removed in 1689 to allow construction of a solid base for the Grand Battery, and it was only in 1921 that they were partially re-excavated and their vaults reconstructed. They probably originally extended between the Elphinstone Tower and the North Gate, and it seems likely that food was taken from the kitchens through a corridor which passed through the first floor of the North Gate. The kitchens now contain a display showing how they would have appeared when in use in the sixteenth century.

The North Gate may contain the earliest visible masonry in the castle, the outer part probably dating from 1381. It was extended inwards and heightened on a number of occasions, but the most extensive works were in 1511-12, when a kitchen to serve the Great Hall was evidently constructed on the first floor, probably under the supervision of the mason, John Lockhart.

*The re-created Great Kitchens.*

# ⑩ The Nether Bailey & Magazines

The Nether Bailey, entered by the North Gate, is a large irregular enclosure occupying a lower terrace to the north of the castle's main area. There was probably never a main entrance to the castle on this side, though there are two small blocked doorways - one on the east and another on the west - which were probably closed when the castle's defences were strengthened in 1689. These doorways could have been used for a variety of purposes, including concealed access in time of siege; that on the west was probably also used for access to the royal gardens.

Within the Nether Bailey are a Guard House and four Powder Magazines, most of which were built in about 1810. Three of the magazines are surrounded by a high wall, are covered by parabolic vaults and had baffled vents in their side walls to contain the impact of any explosion. In 1908 these three magazines were interconnected and converted for use as transit stores. At the far end of the magazine enclosure, the fourth powder magazine was built for the Volunteer Corps raised in 1860. The Nether Bailey also contains the curved wall of a miniature rifle range.

*An aerial view of the castle with the Nether Bailey in the foreground.*

17

# ⑪ The Royal Parks & Gardens

From the Bowling Green Gardens visitors can look down to the remains of the gardens in the valley west of the castle. No-one looking at the royal buildings at Stirling Castle could imagine it as the dour fortress that castles are sometimes thought to be. Nor were the royal amenities limited to the summit of the castle rock; below its walls were hunting parks and gardens which were delightful places of recreation. A hunting forest for the castle existed from at least the early twelfth century, and was enclosed towards the end of that century, making it the first known royal park in Scotland.

That park was apparently directly below the west side of the castle walls, and extended well towards the south. By the early fourteenth century the Old Park had been superseded by a New Park south of Stirling, in the Bannockburn area. However, James IV evidently preferred the situation of the Old Park, and by about 1500 its boundaries were being re-established with ditches and palisaded banks, while animals were brought in to restock it. Something of its character can be understood from references to the wild white cattle which grazed within it by 1509, and to a display of Spanish horsemanship there in the same year.

One advantage of the Old Park was that it was visible from the castle, and the Ladies' Lookout (behind the Palace) was a favourite spot for the ladies of the court to look down on the gardens which formed part of it. James IV was a keen gardener, and acquired many seeds, plants and trees. His gardens were probably on the site of the imposing earthworks still to be seen to the south-west of the castle, and now known as the King's Knot, though in their present form these earthworks date from 1628-9 with extensive nineteenth-century restorations. Later writers speculated that the raised mound at the centre of the earthworks had been the base for King Arthur's round table; that is legend, yet, in view of James IV's interest in the Arthurian legends and his love of tournaments, it is not impossible that there was some reference to Camelot in the layout of the garden which preceded the one whose remains we now see.

*The view across the Royal Gardens from the Ladies' Lookout.*

*A view of the castle in the 1670s, painted by J. Vosterman.*
*(Courtesy of the Smith Art Gallery and Museum, Stirling.)*

# The Story of Stirling Castle

Stirling Castle is one of that small number of buildings that has come to symbolise the spirit of Scotland for Scots and non-Scots alike. Dramatically set at the very heart of the kingdom, on a high volcanic rock, it commands the countryside for many miles around in all directions. Before the marshes to its west were drained and the network of roads and railways around its base was developed, its situation was even more commanding, and whoever possessed the castle was well placed to control all movement throughout the centre of Scotland. Not for nothing was it likened to 'a huge brooch clasping Highlands and Lowlands together'.

There was a favourite royal castle here from at least the twelfth century - and possibly for long before then - and its role in both peace and war is central to much of the story of medieval Scotland.

Without the castle, for example, there would have been no need for William Wallace to fight the battle of Stirling Bridge in 1297, or for Robert I (the Bruce) to fight at Bannockburn in 1314.

However, the magnificent buildings which now crown the castle rock are all later than that, dating mainly from the late 1400s and the 1500s, when the castle was perhaps the most ambitiously planned of the settings for the court of James IV, James V and James VI. Despite several centuries of adaptation to military use after James VI moved south to become James I of England in 1603, the buildings raised for those monarchs survive remarkably well. They offer an unequalled impression of the architectural backdrop against which a dynasty of medieval and Renaissance monarchs both governed their kingdom and made their mark on the European scene.

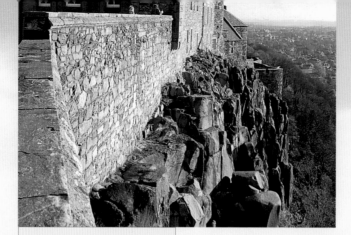

*The west face of the castle rock.*

*Stirling and the River Forth from Dumyat.*

# The Castle Rock

The castle rock came into existence roughly 350 million years ago as a layer of molten rock forced up from a distant volcanic fissure, and which flowed outwards between layers of hard rock before rising upwards at what is now Stirling. By the start of the last Ice Age, about one and a half million years ago, the rock may already have begun to emerge as a significant landscape feature, but it was the movement of ice which fully exposed the edge of the sill. The scouring action of ice sheets, moving from north-west to south-east, created sheer faces along the rock's western side and northern end. As the ice melted, an inlet of the sea formed around the rock, but layers of clay, and then of peat, built up to form vast tracts of marshland to the west of the rock, through which the River Forth meandered out to the gradually withdrawing sea. Confining these marshlands - the Flanders, Blairdrummond and Drip Mosses - were the Ochil Hills to the north-east of the rock, and the Gargunnock and Touch Hills to the south-west.

The Mosses have been drained over the last two centuries, and the resultant rich farmland now presents no barrier to movement. But throughout the Middle Ages the combination of marshes, high hills and a major river restricted communication routes. Until recently many of the main land and water routes running both north-south and east-west through central Scotland had to pass directly below the castle rock, and whoever controlled Stirling controlled much of the country. The combination of an almost impregnable rock site and a location of such high strategic significance made Stirling an irresistible situation for a major castle.

# Legendary Beginnings

It is not known when the castle rock was first occupied and defended. Since prehistoric forts have been found on a number of other hills in the vicinity it is possible there was also an early fort here, though no evidence of this has yet been found. Moving on to the period once known as 'the Dark Ages', even before the end of the Middle Ages some writers were suggesting that Stirling had been a seat of King Arthur, though this was no more than legend. Among more historically acceptable possibilities, the rock could have been a stronghold of a northern enclave of the British people known as the Gododdin, the successors of the tribe called the Votadini by the Romans. But by the seventh century the area had come under the control of the Anglians of Northumbria, and in 654 Penda, King of Mercia (in what is now central England) is said to have chased the Anglian King Oswy as far as a place called Iudeu. Some historians have suggested that Iudeu was Stirling. With the defeat of the Anglian King Ecgfrith by the Pictish King Brude at Nechtansmere, near Forfar, in 685, the area presumably came under Pictish control, until both Picts and Scots were progressively forged into a single state from around the mid-ninth century onwards. As part of this process, it was said in the later Middle Ages that a stronghold here was besieged by Kenneth mac Alpin, who had become King of the Scots in 842.

# The First Certainties

It is only from the early twelfth century that things become more certain. The first definite pointer to the existence of a castle comes at a date between 1107 and 1115, when Alexander I arranged for a castle chapel to be dedicated and endowed. The castle was presumably one of his favourite residences, because he died within it in 1124.

A royal castle like Stirling had to meet a wide range of requirements. Apart from being a place of defence, it was a residence for the king and his court, with a need for both accommodation and entertainment. It also had to house the administrative officers who travelled with the king to assist him in governing the kingdom from wherever he chose to base himself. However, we know little about the layout or appearance of the castle at this date. With the possible exception of the chapel, it is likely that most of the buildings and defensive walls were of timber, earth and thatch.

Later in the century Stirling's continuing importance was demonstrated when, following King William the Lion's capture on a raid into England in 1174, it was one of five castles surrendered to Henry II of England under the Treaty of Falaise as the price of William's freedom. The terms of that humiliating treaty were eventually overturned in 1189, and it was at Stirling Castle that William died in 1214.

*Stirling Castle in its setting.*

*A seal of Alexander I
(1107-24) during whose
reign a castle at
Stirling is first mentioned.*

*A view to the Wallace Monument, on Abbey Craig, from one of the gun embrasures of the Grand Battery. Stirling Bridge and the River Forth are down in the valley below.*

26

# The First Phase of the 'Wars of Independence'

The phase of its history for which Stirling Castle is most widely remembered is the late thirteenth and early fourteenth century, when it played a central role in the resistance to English attempts to dominate Scotland. The accidental death of Alexander III in 1286, followed by the death of his granddaughter and only direct heir, Margaret, 'Maid of Norway', in 1290, left Scotland without a single claimant to the throne, and Edward I of England was called in to adjudicate between the various contenders. Edward briefly stayed at Stirling in 1291 while arrangements were being made for the Scottish nobility to accept his role, and in 1292 at Berwick judgement was given in favour of John Balliol. But after King John refused to support Edward I in his wars with France in 1295, Edward swept north in the following year on a punitive campaign, during which John was deposed. As part of the same campaign Edward took Stirling Castle, and it was the Scottish determination to regain the castle which led to the Battle of Stirling Bridge in 1297. Unfortunately, this famous victory was followed by the loss of the castle to the English in the next year, after the Scottish defeat at Falkirk.

Nevertheless, the Scots were again besieging the castle in 1299, and the English constable, John Sampson, was forced to surrender when no relief appeared. But by 1303 the wheel of fortune had turned yet again, and Stirling was the only significant stronghold remaining in Scottish hands, making Edward I more determined than ever to retake it. He had floating bridges made at King's Lynn, in Norfolk, to allow him to cross the Forth below Stirling and, once at Dunfermline, he started building at least 17 great siege engines. The siege began in April 1304, and eventually the castle's captain, Sir William Oliphant, offered surrender on 20 July, though Edward I insisted that some of the garrison remain within the castle until he had tried out his most favoured siege engine, 'the war wolf', which probably fired heavy stones.

## The Battle of Stirling Bridge, 1297

Early in September the Scottish army, led by William Wallace and Andrew Murray, took up position on Abbey Craig, overlooking the timber bridge over the Forth, a short way upstream of the present bridge. They bided their time, knowing that the English, under the command of the Earl of Surrey, had at some stage to cross that bridge. Eventually, on 11 September, the English began to cross. Wallace and Murray held off until the enemy were well on the bridge, and then they gave the order to charge. The English cavalry, struggling two abreast across the narrow causeway, were caught in the trap. Some were killed outright, others were drowned, and only a lucky few got away. Hugh Cressingham, Edward I of England's Treasurer, was killed and his body skinned. Alas for the Scots, Andrew Murray was badly injured in the battle and died of his wounds that November, and William Wallace lost his next battle against the English, at Falkirk, the following summer.

*A nineteenth-century depiction of the Battle of Stirling Bridge, by William Brassey Hole. (Courtesy of the Scottish National Portrait Gallery.)*

*A statue of William Wallace on the Wallace Monument.*

# The Second Phase of the 'Wars of Independence'

A combination of the death of Edward I in 1307 and the inspired leadership of Robert I led to a rapid improvement in Scottish fortunes. By 1313 only the castles of Stirling, Edinburgh, Berwick and Bothwell remained in English hands, and Robert's younger brother, Edward, laid siege to Stirling, captained by Sir Philip Moubray. However, Edward Bruce lifted the siege on the understanding that the castle would be handed to the Scots if not relieved by the English before Midsummer's Day of 1314. It was Edward II's determination to retain Stirling which led to the Battle of Bannockburn on 23 and 24 June 1314, and which gave the Scots one of their finest victories. By this stage, however, Robert considered that the best policy was to render all castles indefensible, to avoid the risk of their being held against him, and this was done at Stirling after Bannockburn.

As so often, Scottish good fortune was not sustained. Robert I's heir at his death in 1329 was his five-year-old son, David II, and in 1332 the son of John Balliol, Edward, took advantage of the new king's youth to invade the kingdom, with the support of Edward III of England and those Scottish nobles earlier dispossessed for disloyalty by Robert I. Stirling was again under English control from at least 1336, when its warden was Sir Thomas Rokeby, and much building and strengthening work was then carried out. Andrew Murray (whose father, also Andrew Murray, was Wallace's co-leader at Stirling Bridge) laid an abortive siege in 1337, though it was only in 1342 that it was eventually re-taken for the Scots, by Robert the Steward.

*The equestrian statue of Robert I at Bannockburn, with Stirling Castle in the background.*

# The Battle of Bannockburn, 1314

The Scots had given the English a deadline of Midsummer's Day to relieve their beleaguered garrison in the Stirling Castle or have them surrender. Edward II took up the challenge and crossed the River Tweed on 17 June at the head of a 20,000-strong army. King Robert (the Bruce) mustered his smaller force near Bannock Burn, a little to the south of Stirling, and waited. On Sunday 23 June, the English vanguard, under the Earl of Hereford, approached the Scottish lines and charged. One of the earliest encounters was between the Bruce himself and Henry de Bohun, and the sight of their King splitting open the skull of the Earl of Hereford's nephew with his battleaxe moved the Scots to repulse the attack. The two sides then drew back to their positions.

Bruce would have retired altogether from the fray had he not received word during the night that the English camp were utterly demoralised by the day's events. On the following morning, Midsummer's Day, the Scottish schiltrons (large formations of pike-wielding infantry) advanced and wreaked havoc. The English, finding themselves trapped between the Bannock Burn and the River Forth, were thrown into utter confusion. Many were drowned, others were cut down either by their pursuers or by their own comrades desperate to get away. Edward II contrived to reach the safety of Stirling Castle and eventually escaped back to England. Robert the Bruce had pulled off one of the greatest military victories in Scottish history.

*The Battle of Bannockburn, depicted in the 15th-century* Scotichronicon. *In the foreground Bruce slays de Bohun; in the background is Stirling Castle. (Courtesy of the Master & Fellows of Corpus Christi College, Cambridge.)*

*An aerial view of the castle from the north-west.*

# The Castle in the Later Middle Ages

In the later Middle Ages there are many records of major building work, and there is more than ever a sense that Stirling and its castle were at the heart of the nation's affairs. Robert the Steward succeeded David II to the throne in 1371, as Robert II, and during his time much attention was paid to the castle's defences. Indeed, the earliest part of the castle to survive above ground, the core of the North Gate, was probably under construction during his reign, in 1381.

A role which was to become increasingly important for the castle was that of royal nursery. After James I returned from England in 1424 (he had been a captive there since 1406), he granted the castle to his queen as part of her marriage settlement, and this was also to be done by many of his successors on the throne. Less attractively, Stirling was where James I settled some of his scores against those he felt had done too little to obtain his release. The main culprit was his uncle, Robert Duke of Albany, who had been Governor of the kingdom in his absence, but as he had died at Stirling Castle in 1420, James' wrath was instead directed against his son, Murdoch Duke of Albany. Following a session of parliament at Stirling on 24 May 1425, Murdoch and two of his sons were beheaded on the castle hill. James I's continuing high-handed behaviour was a factor in his assassination in 1437, after which there is a tradition that Queen Joan smuggled the six-year-old James II to Stirling in a chest. However, she herself was to undergo a period of undignified imprisonment within her castle after her second marriage two years later.

Although little building is recorded during the reign of James II, Stirling was still a much-used royal residence. In 1449, the year of the King's marriage to Mary of Guelders, a niece of the Duke of Burgundy, the castle was the setting for a tournament in which the main protagonists were two Burgundian knights, Simon and Jacques de Lalain, and two members of the Douglas family. Three years later, however, the head of the Douglas family, William, eighth Earl of Douglas, was murdered by James II's own hand within the castle. This act was regarded as particularly reprehensible since the Earl had been invited to the castle under the King's special protection, in order to persuade him to break alliances felt to be against the royal interest. The King was unable to control his anger when Douglas refused to comply. Traditionally this murder is located in the King's Old Building, which in fact had not been built by then.

James III commissioned more building than his father. Accounts show he was at work on an unidentified 'white tower' in 1463 and on the castle walls in 1467, and there were major works on the Chapel between 1467 and 1469. In addition, he was enlarging the royal collection of artillery, some of which was cast within the castle gun house in 1475. Alas, none of his building work survives in identifiable form. By the sixteenth century, in the writings of Robert Lindsay of Pitscottie, James III was also said to have been the monarch who built the Great Hall, employing his supposed favourite, Thomas Cochrane, though it now looks certain that it was his son, James IV, who built the Hall.

James III was on poor terms with his wife, Margaret of Denmark, in the later years of their marriage, and she spent the last three years of her life at the castle, largely apart from her husband. With her at Stirling was the young Duke of Rothesay, the future James IV, and he remained there after his mother's death in 1486. Two years later he was persuaded to leave the castle to join the magnates who had risen against his father, and this was probably the most important factor in James III's defeat at Sauchieburn and his subsequent assassination. When James IV succeeded to the throne, he confessed his part in his father's death to the head of the castle's chapel. From then on he is said to have worn an iron belt around his waist as penance and evidence of his deep remorse.

*A stained-glass window bearing the arms of the Earl of Douglas in the King's Old Building.*

# The Burgh of Stirling

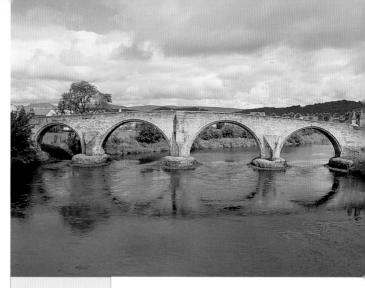

A royal castle did not exist in isolation. Many people were required to service the needs of its occupants, though not all of those lived within the castle itself. Additionally, the protection afforded by a major stronghold, particularly when it was set at the junction of important trade routes, acted as a magnet to craftsmen and those who wished to sell their goods in peace. Consequently, urban settlements grew up around castles, and at Stirling the natural place for this burgh was along the sloping main approach to the castle. As early as the reign of David I (1124-53), the developing settlement here was given the privilege of royal protection, and during his reign - if not before - there was a parish church to meet the spiritual needs of its people.

*Stirling Bridge.*

*Holy Rude parish church.*

Stirling has retained many fine buildings from before the time of its modern expansion. Grandest of all is the parish church of the Holy Rude, which was rebuilt in two principal campaigns starting around 1414 and 1507, resulting in one of the most imposing of Scotland's great late medieval burgh churches. The burgh also had several other churches, including friaries for the Dominicans and Observant Franciscans, the chapels of at least five hospitals, and the Augustinian abbey of Cambuskenneth in the valley to the east.

Of these churches only HolyRude and Cambuskenneth Abbey still have visible remains, though something of the Dominican church is known from excavations. Other partly pre-Reformation buildings include the four-arched bridge over the Forth, and parts of the town wall. The present bridge is probably largely of the sixteenth century, though we know that the earliest bridges here were of timber, and a short way upstream. The remaining parts of the wall along the south and west sides of the burgh date mainly from a decision by the burgh council to provide defences in 1547.

*Cambuskenneth Abbey beside the River Forth, with Stirling Castle in the background.*

The burgh also has several early houses, including two of the finest aristocratic town houses in Scotland. The most prestigious situations for such houses were around the market area (now known as Broad Street) and on the road to the castle. Mar's Wark, which commands the top end of the market, is the surviving wing of a quadrangular Renaissance palace started in 1570 for John, first Earl of Mar, who became Regent of the kingdom in 1571. Argyll's Lodging, on Castle Wynd, incorporates fragments of sixteenth-century houses, but assumed its present form in campaigns of the 1630s and 1670s for the first Earl of Stirling and the ninth Earl of Argyll. Cowane's Hospital, on the south side of the parish church, was built as an almshouse with money bequeathed in 1633 by the merchant John Cowane. Cowane's family house also survives in a ruined state where the road leading down to the bridge joins St Mary's Wynd.

*Mar's Wark.*

*Argyll's Lodging.*

# James IV's Sumptuous Royal Residence

Despite the inauspicious start to his reign, James IV was perhaps the most attractive member of the Stewart dynasty, and Stirling was a principal centre for the brilliant court which he assembled around himself. Through the buildings he erected we see how a fortress of formidable strength could also accommodate a sumptuous royal residence, and it was against this background that he was able to show himself to the rest of Europe as a prince of the Renaissance. Rather unfairly, however, his encouragement of learning within the castle is often best remembered for his patronage of the Italian scholar, John Damian, who undertook alchemical experiments to turn base metals into gold. Damian is also said to have tried to fly to France from the walls of Stirling in 1507, using wings of his own making, and to have concluded that the inevitable result was because the hen feathers he used had a more natural affinity with the midden than with the skies!

James IV was Scotland's greatest builder of palatial architecture, carrying out major works at Holyrood, Edinburgh, Falkland, Linlithgow and Rothesay, though it is at Stirling that we see the most complete expression of his architectural ambitions. It was probably James IV who started to have the main royal enclave of the castle, the Inner Close, laid out to the plan we still see. He built his own residence, the King's Old Building, on the west side of the Close, with the Great Hall facing it on the east, and he established a college of priests as Scotland's Chapel Royal, probably within the chapel his father had improved on the north side of the Close. He also built the Forework, a great frontispiece containing the main entrance to the castle. In addition, he may have remodelled an earlier range as a residence for his queen, Margaret Tudor, around the time of their marriage in 1503, and we must assume that he would have built much else - including perhaps a new chapel - if he had not been killed at the Battle of Flodden in 1513 when only 40.

*A reconstruction of the Forework in its original state (David Simon).*

A reconstruction of the King's Old Building as it may have originally looked (David Simon).

# James V's Palace

James V was crowned in the Chapel at Stirling 12 days after his father's death, on 21 September 1513. He was only 17 months old. His subsequent upbringing cannot have been a happy time for him, as various magnates squabbled over control of the royal person. By the age of 16 he had effectively established his own authority and, perhaps partly in reaction against his English mother, his own horizons were distinctly European. As early as 1517 it had been agreed in the Treaty of Rouen that he was to have a French bride, though François I of France was less enthusiastic when the time came to honour his agreement. Eventually, in 1536, James V went in person to France to claim a bride, and was rewarded with the Princess Madeleine, who was to

*The statue of James V on his Palace.*

die within six months of the marriage. For his second wife he took the more robust daughter of the Duke of Guise-Lorraine, Mary of Guise. To house his second French queen, James V built the magnificent Palace at Stirling. A number of French details show that James had taken a close interest in the buildings of his first father-in-law whilst visiting France, and we also know that he had several French masons in his service. James V's court at Stirling must have been as vibrant as that of his father, and it is particularly pleasing to think that at least some of the exquisite church music of Robert Carver was composed for the Chapel Royal. But the fifth James's life was even briefer than his father's, since he died in 1542 at the age of 30, broken by the disastrous defeat of his army by the English at Solway Moss, leaving a female baby to succeed him.

*A winged cherub.*

*A corbel head.*

*A crossbow-man.*

*The Devil.*

*Details of the splendid carving on the Palace.*

*A reconstruction of the Queen's Bed Chamber in the Palace in the time of Queen Mary of Guise (David Simon).*

# The Castle & Queen Mary

Mary was crowned as Queen of Scots on 9 September 1543 within the Chapel Royal, a ceremony said dismissively by Henry VIII of England's representative to have been carried out with 'not very costlie' ceremonial. Henry VIII saw the marriage of his own son, Prince Edward, to the infant queen as his best hope of reviving English claims to Scotland, and the marriage was agreed under the Treaty of Greenwich in 1543. But many in Scotland doubted English assurances that Scottish independence would be respected and by 1548, after two further phases of warfare with England, it was decided to send the infant queen to France for marriage to the heir to the French throne, who succeeded as François II in 1559.

*The French Spur.*

During Mary's absence in France, Scotland was frequently a battleground between those who wished the country to move towards a closer alliance with Protestant England, and those who preferred a relationship with Catholic France. Various major artillery fortifications were raised by both sides, and at Stirling we now realise that, embodied within later structures, there are significant remains of a particularly important system of outer defences, (including the French Spur) which were almost certainly built for Mary of Guise in the 1550s.

Mary Queen of Scots returned to her Scottish kingdom in 1561, after the death of both her mother and her French husband, and found a country that had become Protestant while she remained Catholic. The Chapel Royal at Stirling was apparently the only palace chapel still fitted out for Catholic worship; even so, at her first service within the castle her half-brother, Lord James Stewart, together with the Earl of Argyll, physically attacked the officiating clergy. Soon afterwards the Queen had another misfortune at Stirling, narrowly escaping death when her bed curtains caught fire.

The happiest event associated with Mary at the castle was the baptism of her son, Prince James, on 17 December 1566, although she was by then estranged from her husband, Lord Darnley. After the ceremony, which was carried out with Catholic ritual, using a golden font provided by Elizabeth I of England, the celebrations lasted for a further two days. The second day was largely taken up with audiences for ambassadors, while on the third there was a lavish banquet with an Arthurian theme. The high point of the celebrations was the allegorical siege of an enchanted castle on the open ground in front of the castle, followed by a display of fireworks and artillery. In all of this Mary was determined to show that Scotland could rival the most ambitious celebrations to be seen at any of the European courts, even if she had to borrow from the merchants of Edinburgh to pay for it.

*A reconstruction of the 'pretend' siege of an enchanted castle played out in front of the castle in December 1566 as part of the baptismal celebrations for Prince James (David Simon).*

# The Castle & King James VI

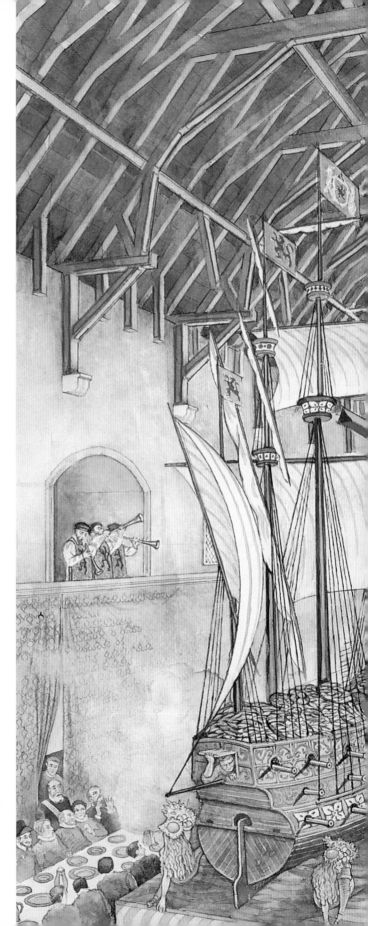

Mary was forced to abdicate on 24 July 1567. She was succeeded by the year-old James VI, who was crowned in Stirling parish church five days later. Much of James' childhood was passed within Stirling Castle, where he was taught by the formidable scholar, George Buchanan, who did not scruple to advise the King what James thought about his mother. As usual with royal minorities, James became a focus for rival factions. There were attacks on the castle while the king was in residence in 1571 and 1578; he was taken there as a virtual prisoner after the Ruthven Raid in 1582, and there was a further siege in 1585.

Reports on the structural state of the castle from James VI's reign suggest that lack of maintenance had led to some buildings being in a state of pending collapse. One of these was the Chapel Royal, which was both in a poor state and in an inconvenient position, and James VI's chief architectural contribution to the castle was its rebuilding to an elegant design in 1594. The reason for this was the baptism of Prince Henry, the first son born to James and Queen Anne of Denmark. By this stage it was certain that the 60-year-old Elizabeth I of England would have no children, and it was now the turn of a monarch of Scotland to have claims on the English throne. In producing a son, and giving him a name favoured by the English royal house, James was therefore offering the prospect of continuity to both England and Scotland. The celebrations were duly magnificent. One of the centrepieces of the banquet held afterwards in the Great Hall was a splendid ship which brought in a variety of fish, and which was apparently such a fine piece that it was preserved into the eighteenth century.

*The Chapel Royal.*

*A reconstruction of the King's Presence Chamber within the Palace in the time of James VI (David Simon).*

*A reconstruction of the baptismal celebrations in the Great Hall for Prince Henry in 1594 (David Simon).*

41

The Royal Gardens as remodelled for Charles I.

# The Monarchs Depart

James VI's ambition to succeed to the English throne was fulfilled on the death of Elizabeth I in 1603. On moving south he said he would make many 'homecomings' to his Scottish kingdom, but he found it surprisingly easy to rule Scotland from England and only made one visit, in 1617. Various works were carried out within the castle to make it suitable for that visit. Even more was done before the visit expected from Charles I following his succession in 1625, though it was only in 1633 that he found opportunity for his Scottish coronation.

With such a reduced royal presence there was little need for major building works at the Scottish palaces, and from this period onwards it is the military aspect of the castle which once again became paramount. Little was done at the time of Charles I's second visit to Scotland in 1641, when he was at loggerheads with the Covenanting party in Scotland, and England was on the verge of civil war. Following his execution in 1649, his son was declared king in Scotland, as Charles II, and the English parliamentary army came north on a punitive campaign in 1650. As part of this, General Monk took the castle by siege in 1651, and the marks made by his artillery are still to be seen on some buildings.

After his restoration to the English throne in 1660, Charles II had little inclination to revisit Scotland, but did agree to rebuild Holyrood as the Scottish royal palace in the 1670s. He also sent his brother, James Duke of Albany and York, to Scotland at a time when his open Catholicism was causing offence in England. James visited the castle on 3-4 February 1681, but its buildings were in no fit state for him to stay there. The Duke succeeded to the Scottish and English thrones as James VII and II in 1685, but was forced to flee in 1688, being succeeded by his daughter Mary and her husband, William of Orange. However, James VII never abdicated, and he and his son and grandsons were to provide a focus of rival loyalty for over a century. Their supporters were known as Jacobites, from the Latin *Jacobus* meaning James.

*Wall decoration from the Chapel Royal showing the cipher of Charles I and the Honours of Scotland (the Crown Jewels).*

# The Jacobite Threat

No sooner had a Scottish convention proclaimed William and Mary as joint monarchs in March 1689 than rebellion broke out under the leadership of John Graham of Claverhouse, Viscount Dundee. Although this was eventually suppressed, it created concern about the weakness of the Scottish castles, and improvements were made to Stirling by closing off two lesser entrances, and by providing artillery mountings on the more vulnerable east side. Naturally enough, such emergency measures paid little respect to the castle's architectural qualities, and from this point onwards military needs were increasingly given greater weight than aesthetic considerations.

If many Scots felt they had no part in the deposition of James VII, they felt even more alienated after the childless Queen Anne came to the throne in 1702 and the English parliament decided that the children of Sophia, Electress of Hanover, were to succeed her. A further incentive to disloyalty was the Union of the Kingdoms. Under James VI, Charles I, Charles II, James VII and William and Mary, Scotland and England were only united by the fact that they had the same monarch; but in 1707 it was decided that the kingdoms should be themselves united, and the last session of the Scottish parliament was closed on 28 April. Although James VII had died in 1701, his son, Prince James, known as the Old Pretender, continued his family's claim to the throne, and following the Act of Union he persuaded Louis XIV of France to provide a fleet and army to invade Scotland. This fleet sailed into the Firth of Forth on 23 March 1708 and, despite the fact that the anticipated popular rising did not materialise, it was decided that the principal castles had to be strengthened.

At Stirling the strengthening was carried out between 1708 and 1714, to the designs of Captain Theodore Dury, the military engineer for Scotland. His first proposals, for simply enclosing the area in front of the castle, were criticised by Captain Obryan, a fellow engineer, and their superior, Talbot Edwards, was called on to arbitrate. The scheme eventually

*A sentry box and the French Spur in the Outer Defences.*

adopted incorporated parts of the outworks built for Mary of Guise in the 1550s. The progress of work may have been interrupted by John, sixth Earl of Mar, the governor of the castle and a keen architectural connoisseur, who wished to improve both the royal lodgings and his own accommodation. However, Mar's involvement with the castle was soon to be ended. Following what he regarded as a snub by the new Hanoverian dynasty, in 1715 he instigated a rising on behalf of the deposed Stewart line, raising the standard of the Old Pretender at Braemar on 6 September. Owing to his own inadequacies as a general - he lost the Battle of Sheriffmuir when he should have won it - he was soon in exile in Paris, and while there he found some solace drawing up more elaborate schemes for remodelling the Palace for a restored Stewart dynasty.

The new defences of the castle were tested as part of the last major Jacobite rising, in 1745-6, led by Prince Charles Edward Stewart (Bonnie Prince Charlie) on behalf of his father, the Old Pretender. A few shots were fired as his army marched southwards in 1745, but on his return north in 1746 he laid siege to the castle from the adjacent Gowan Hill, only to find that the commander of the castle, General Blakeney, made short work of his artillery emplacements once he opened fire from the batteries created on that side of the castle in 1689.

*A proposal drawn up by the exiled Earl of Mar
after the 1715 Rising for the remodelling of the Palace.*

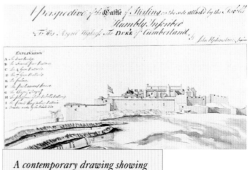

*A contemporary drawing showing
the site of the last siege in 1746.*

# The Castle in Recent Times

Despite such occasional rude awakenings, Stirling Castle was rapidly becoming a military back-water. There was no reason to carry out more than minimal maintenance of its great buildings, and in 1777, for example, when part of a fine ceiling in the king's lodging fell, the rest was simply removed. Such architecture was no longer greatly valued, and there was little money to pay for work which was not militarily necessary. While this may now be deemed regrettable, the more positive aspect of the situation is that lack of interest meant there were no great schemes of rebuilding, and adaptations were kept to the essential minimum.

The situation changed at the end of the century, on the outbreak of warfare with Revolutionary and Napoleonic France. In 1794 Stirling was the rendezvous for Campbell of Lochnell's mustering of the Duke of Argyll's Highland regiment (one of the two component elements of what was to become the regiment of the Argyll and Sutherland Highlanders, and which was eventually to have the castle as its base after the two elements were united in 1881). Soon afterwards, there was a drive to provide accommodation at all of the major castles, which at Stirling was achieved by inserting floors and walls in the Great Hall to create barrack rooms. From then on, Stirling was to be home to varying numbers of soldiers, and the castle was increasingly adapted to meet their needs. The royal buildings - and many lesser buildings as well - had to respond to these changed requirements, though this did at least ensure that they were preserved. Additionally, several new buildings were raised, from the Main Guard House and Fort Major's House in the Outer Close, to the magazines in the Nether Bailey, and these are now valued as an integral part of the castle's architectural history.

*One of the barrack rooms in the subdivided Great Hall.*

But even while military requirements were met, there was growing appreciation of the castle's architectural qualities during the nineteenth century. By 1849 it was felt to be worth a visit by Queen Victoria, who thought it was 'extremely grand'. It was also admired by Robert Billings, who included views in his influential publication on the *Baronial and Ecclesiastical Antiquities of Scotland*, published between 1845 and 1852. Billings was himself called on to rebuild the damaged parts of the King's Old Building after a fire in 1855, and here - perhaps for the first time - we see an attempt to respect and reflect the castle's historic ambience. Nevertheless, the army's priority still had to be the accommodation of its soldiers, though there was a shift of emphasis after 1906, when King Edward VII asked that maintenance of the buildings be transferred from the War Office to the Office of Works.

*The Prince's Walk and Forework gatehouse when the castle was in military use.*

*The north front of the King's Old Building as remodelled by Billings after 1855.*

With the cooperation of the War Office, the change of responsibility in 1906 encouraged a more sympathetic climate for the care of the castle's historic structures and, where possible, works were carried out in a way that allowed their inherent qualities to be appreciated. Yet further changes became possible when the castle ceased to be the military depot for the Argyll and Sutherland Highlanders in 1964, though some might have felt that, with the loss of both its monarchs

*The memorial to the Argyll and Sutherland Highlanders on the Castle Esplanade.*

and its permanent complement of soldiers, there was a risk of the castle forfeiting something of its *raison d'être*. However, in recent years, major works of improvement have been instigated, including the restoration of the Great Hall. These permit what is arguably the finest complex of late medieval and Renaissance royal buildings in Scotland to be seen to greater advantage, and hopefully without any sense of sterile lack of purpose.

## FURTHER READING

H J Crawford 'Stirling Castle in art', *Transactions of the Stirlingshire Natural History Association* (1934-5)

John Dunbar *The Stirling Heads*, 2nd edition (1975)

Richard Fawcett *Stirling Castle* (1995)

Michael Lynch 'Queen Mary's Triumph: the baptismal celebrations at Stirling in December 1566', *Scottish Historical Review*, vol 69 (1990)

Charles McKean *Stirling and the Trossachs* (RIAS guide) (1985)

Royal Commission on the Ancient and Historical Monuments of Scotland *Inventory of Stirlingshire* (1963)

Eric Stair-Kerr *Stirling Castle*, 2nd edition (1928)

Chris Tabraham *Scotland's Castles* (1997)

Chris Tabraham & Doreen Grove *Fortress Scotland and the Jacobites* (1995)